EDDA USA

EVER AFTER HIGH – WRITE FABLEOUS FAIRYTALES
© 2016 Mattel Inc.

Author: Judy Katschke
Layout and cover design: Olafur Gunnar Gudlaugsson
Printed in Canada

Distributed by Macmillan

ISBN: 978-1-94078-749-7

www.eddausa.com

INTRODUCTION

To the students of Ever After High the most spelltacular books are the ones that rock their worlds.

For hexample, a riddle-iculously funny story turns Madeline Hatter's world upside down. A fairytale enchants Duchess Swan while C.A. Cupid feels the love in a poem.

Their tastes in tales may be as different as a dragon and a dormouse – but guess what? They all share one thing in common: they all enjoy a good story. They also know that storytelling takes imagination and skill. And like dragon-slaying, spell-casting and tea brewing, skills can be sharpened with spelltacular games and hexercises.

So let the storytelling begin – for you! Turn the page, say hello to some BFFA's – and begin writing your own happily ever after…

CORE OF A STORY

"The most spelltacular stories are the ones that begin with 'Once Upon a Time' and end with 'Happily Ever After.' But the core of the story – the part that makes a story a story – is the juiciest part of all!"

Apple White

To get to the core of your story you first need to know what's fairy-often inside:

Characters: The stars of your story, like kings, queens, wicked stepmothers and hunters. All characters in your story are important but the main character is the hero of your tale. It helps to have the reader like your hero. And since you'll be spending time with your main character while writing the story, it's important for you to like her too.

Setting: Where the action in your story takes place. Is it a lush forest, filled with woodland creatures? Or a tiny village where candy-covered cottages stand? The better you describe your setting, the better your reader will imagine your world. And with stories imagination rules!

With these steps I know you'll be writing your own story in the bat of a unicorn's eyelash.

Plot: That's what your story is about and what moves it forward. A hexcellent plot keeps your reader reading. It can have suspense, comedy and conflict. Conflict is a problem in your story to be solved.

Resolution: The Happily Ever After. This is when your hero or main character solves her problem through brains, luck or Apple's favorite – magic!

There's a bushel of different story styles out there. So like the most hexquisite apples on a tree you always have your pick!

STORY FRIENDS FUR-EVER

"When I say I can communicate with animals, I talk the talk. Ask any deer, rabbit, hedgehog or Dodo – they'll tell you it's true. It's no wonderland that when I have to pen a story they always star animals, animals and more animals!"

Ashlynn Ella

Want to write your own critter-ary masterpiece? Check out some of Ashlynn's ideas to get started:

ONE Create an imaginary animal and describe it from head to tail. Is it covered with purple feathers or fuzz? Does it have twisted horns and flat feet? How does it walk or fly? Is he a pet – or a threat?

TWO Pretend to interview a chatty critter for your school paper. What do bears really do when they hibernate? Why do mice get such a bad rap? And what about divacorns? Are they truly divas?

THREE Did you ever receive a letter from a far-away 'pet-pal?' You can if you write one yourself.

Soon you'll find out writing about animals is easier than you think. Just put yourself inside their furry heads, understand their worlds and as Ashlynn suggests – always finish your story before midnight!

A PURR-FECT MYSTERY

"I know curiosity killed the cat but I am a little curious …and proud of it. Is it any wonder a puzzling mystery is the purrr-fect story for me to read – and write?"

Kitty Cheshire

What's Kitty Cheshire's fave way to start a mystery? From scratch, of course! And like most magical spells, most mystery stories have a formula with a few key ingredients:

Like the most magical spells most mystery stories have a formula.

A Puzzler: To figure out 'the who' in 'whodunnit' your story needs a main character, determined to put the puzzle pieces together. She can be a professional sleuth or a simple soul with a curious streak.

Suspects: Characters that might have caused the problem your investigator is trying to solve. There can be one suspect or several. Kitty doesn't love following rules but she loves following the rule of three which suggests that things are always better when they come in threes!

Suspense: Hexciting scenes to keep your reader guessing – if possible until the very end.

Clues: Hints along the way to help your investigator solve the mystery. They can be seen, like pawprints leading away from a smashed vase. Or heard, like a 'secret' conversation that isn't a secret anymore. And since Kitty's ancestors loved a good fish, there's always a red herring in her tale. That's a clue that leads the detectives in the wrong direction.

Resolution: The end of the story when all the pieces of the puzzle come together to solve the mystery.

To Kitty, a mystery story is the cat's meow … and the next best thing to pulling a prank!

GIGGLE DEE-DEE!

"What do I love more than hats, Chemythstry and the sweetest enchanting tea? A wonderlandful laugh, of course. So while I'm spending time in my dad's tea shop waiting for the charm-blossom, spritz fizzle or chocolate rhubarb tea to seep, I'm also sharpening my charmedy-writing skills!"

Madeline Hatter

Madeline is quite the comedian, which is why a funny story is her cup of tea. If you have maddeningly funny ideas brewing inside your head, try writing a comedy too. It can be as easy as straw-fairy cream pie as long as you pull a few things out of your own hat:

First put yourself in a silly mood. If you're not feeling it, look in a mirror and make faces. Or watch a comedy movie or TV show for a good giggle. If those don't work, grab the nearest Dodo feather and tickle your toes. It works for Madeline!

If you have mad-funny ideas brewing in your head, write a comedy.

Once you feel tea-rifically silly it's time to come up with funny ideas. Make a list of things that make you laugh. Or take an everyday situation and hexagerate. Got a new hat? What if it gave you the power to read minds? Got a new cat? What if he's Hex Factor material when playing the keyboard? Is the lumpy pea soup in the school Castleteria turning everyone ogre-green?

Be as crown-over-heels as you can be. And remember to include a beginning, middle and end because a funny story is still a story. But the most important thing to remember? Don't be mean or hurt anyone's feelings for a laugh. Because, as Madeline would agree, "Honest to madness – nobody likes a Dormouse Downer!"

MOTHER GOOSEBUMPS

"What does this dark fairy like more than writing cheerhexes? Writing wicked-spooky stories fun enough to tell at sleepovers ... if I ever get invited to one."

Faybelle Thorn

When Faybelle is ready to write a spooky story she never wings it. Instead she conjures up a fairy-helpful set of spellbinding steps:

Start by thinking what's spooky to you. Flowers chasing you through the garden? Growing fur on a cold day? Getting a membership to the witches' curse-of-the-month-club?

Another way to think spooky thoughts is to ask yourself 'what if?' What if your little brother came home from the orthodontist, not with braces, but with fangs? What if your summer camp was built on the grounds of an old dragon cave? What if your new cell phone called your BFFA's – and villains?

Start by thinking what's spooky to you.

When you have your ideas, toss in some fairy-scary villains or monsters, plus a hero to whom the spooky stuff happens. Set up the scary parts early on in your story then write a cauldronful of un-hexpected nail-biting scenes building up to a Scarily Ever After!

You don't have to be a villain like Faybelle to heart a scary story. And most of all – you should never be too scared to write!

ONCE UPON A RHYME

*"Okay, so I'm no archery superstar like my dad Cupid.
But when it comes to giving advice of the love-kind,
I'm one straight shooter. That's why when it comes to
stories, this serious romantic aims straight for poems!"*

C.A. Cupid

The best place to find a rhyme? On the tip of your tongue!

Let's say you want to rhyme the word 'fairy.' Go through the alphabet replacing 'f' with different letters, one by one. Then put them all together in a poem. Hexample: "That fairy's so hairy it's totally scary!'

One hexercise is rewriting 'roses are red, violets are blue.' Like, 'Dragons are swift, snails are slow. I like you more than you'll ever know!"

Some of the most hexcellent poems don't even rhyme.

Some of the most hexcellent poems don't even rhyme. And some like 'haiku' are just a few words. To be hexact: five syllables in the first line, seven in the second and five in the third:

My friend is Lizzie (5)
She plays a game of croquet (7)
Until she's dizzy! (5)

A limerick is a short poem with a strong beat. They can be wonderifically silly like this one about a certain guy C.A. Cupid knows:

There once was a Rebel named Sparrow
Who could never shoot an arrow.
But when he rocked out,
His fans would shout,
From now until tomorrow!

There are fairy-many types of poems to read and to write. What's the best kind? The ones written by you!

FAIRYTALE FORMULA

"Many fairytales have happy endings – but don't get my feathers ruffled. Thanks to my mom, the Swan Queen, I'm doomed for an Unhappily Ever After (honk if you think that stinks). Maybe that's why writing a new story always rules!"

Duchess Swan

If you've ever dreamed of writing your own fairytale, check out some things that come up once-upon-a-time again:

Fairytales usually begin with Once Upon a Time or Long Ago and Far Away. This lets you know a fairytale is about to begin.

Many have settings in make-believe lands with castles and enchanted forests and lakes. They also star some fantastical characters like trolls, giants and pixies.

Fairytales often star queens, kings, princesses, princess and sometimes duchesses. Most have hearts of gold unlike the banes of their hexistence – villains. And what's a fairytale without a witch, evil queen or grumpy ogre?

Fairytales usually begin with Once Upon a Time or Long Ago and Far Away.

Hexes are cast, wishes are granted, good wins over evil and everyone lives Happily Ever After ... maybe even Duchess Swan!

RAP IT UP!

"My dad Humpty Dumpty was a good egg but a bit off the wall. But I, Humphrey Dumpty, refuse to let my bummer of a family story get in the way of telling my own. And the way I choose to do it is through rap!"

Humphrey Dumpty

A rap is like a poem with a beat. It's also meant to be spoken out loud or performed, because raps are usually from the heart.

Humphrey's raps might sound like they come from the top of his head, but like a lot of things worth doing it takes work. When Humphrey wants to come up with a rap, the first thing he does is hatch ideas, usually about important things on his mind:

It's hard to be an egghead when you're misunderstood.

Apple White walked by – and again I'm shell-shocked!

Why didn't all the king's men use glue?

Once Humphrey has the idea he finds the beat by tapping, clapping or working it out on an instrument. If those don't work, try beatboxing. Beatboxing is when you use your mouth to imitate drums and other instruments.

A rap is like a poem with a beat and is usually from the heart

With the beat in place, Humphrey tells his story, either in rhyme or without, making sure to add a hextreme hook. A hook is a chorus of your rap like Humphrey's fave, "Throw your eggs in the air like you just don't care!"

When you put them all together you don't just have a story. That's a rap!

JOURNEY TO JOURNALING

"As Ever After High's aspiring writer I know everyone's stories, but not everyone's secrets. That's because secrets were meant to be ... secret. My own secret thoughts? They're tucked safely away inside my brilliantly-spelltastic Mirror Journal!"

Holly O'Hair

A journal may sound just like a diary but they're spritely different. A diary is a report of what happened during your day: the pop quiz you had in Geograph-fairy, whom you ate with in the Castleteria, the potion you whipped up in Throne Economics, and more.

Unlike a diary, a journal is a total wild card. That means you can write whatever you wish. Got a crush but don't want to spill? Tell your journal. Dream of winning the Spell Bee but too scared to compete? Don't fright – write! A journal is a place to write thoughts, feelings, memories, plans, lists, even your wildest dreams. And on days when you draw a blank, just a few prompts can shuffle your imagination such as:

"If I were Queen, I'd ..."

"Before I grow up I want to ..."

"If I could turn myself into anything else it would be ..."

Remember, only you get to write in your journal so journal-writing can break all the rules. And since crafty is cool, Holly styles her journal cover and pages with eye-popping stickers, drawings, sparkles, feathers, photos and paw-prints!

Journals can be shared or kept super-secret private in a carefully selected hiding place. Holly keeps hers high in a tower where no one can reach it. Unless, of course, you have locks like hers!

GREAT ADVENTURES

"The books I crave are the ones hexploding with adventure. Maybe because when I'm not reading about adventures, I'm living them. A school of razor eels swimming my way? No problem. Being backed against a wall by a dragon with bonfire breath? On it. My adventures may be unpredictable but when it comes to writing my own story -- I know hexactly where to begin."

Darling Charming

For Darling, beginning means freeing her imagination from its steely armor to create a story idea. Many adventures star a hero with a goal. Maybe she's saving her town from a villain who cast a curse. Maybe she's on a quest to find a secret treasure before someone else does. Maybe the hero will have something special to help her conquer danger, like super-strength, wisdom or speed – or a helpful sidekick like Darling's horse Sir Gallopad!

Once a hero is in place it's time to choose your villains. Will he or she try to keep your hero from reaching her goal? Do they have powers too? It's all up to you!

After you've decided all of this, it's time to choose a setting. This is where the adventure will take place. It can be anywhere from close to home to somewhere faraway and hexotic.

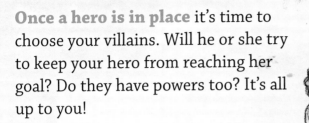

An adventurous hero will fairy-often find herself in a cauldronful of crown-spinning, nail-biting dilemmas. But if she's anything like Darling she won't distress. Instead she'll do whatever she can to triumph over evil and save the day happily ever after. As Darling tells her brothers, "Life is a big adventure – so make your story one too!"

STORY SOUP

"What's cooking? If you're me, Ginger Breadhouse – just about everything! Spelly Donuts, Sugared Gingerbread Men (no relation) and Pasta Primafairy are just a few of my charming recipes. But did you know there's a recipe for the most Ever After Awesome Story told? It's true. And the ingredients are no secret!"

Ginger Breadhouse

Did you know there's a recipe for the most Ever After Awesome Story told?

For a well-crafted story, no matter the kind, combine the following ingredients:

ONE A hextremely hexciting hook to grab the readers.

TWO One cauldronful of delicious spicy characters.

THREE A dash of page-turning suspense.

FOUR A sprinkle of humor, because even spooky stories need an occasional cackle-break.

FIVE Mix ingredients well and top with a hexciting Happily Ever After.

This story recipe makes unlimited servings so share immediately with friends. Because, like the yummy Tea Lime Pie that Ginger has cooling on her windowsill, stories are meant to be shared. So the next time you crave something totally yummy, cook up a little magic. Be like Ginger – and cook up a story!

STORY GAMES AND HEXERCISES

Writing stories can be totally heart-tastic but ideas don't always come easy. What if writing your story becomes more of a grind than a spellebration? Do you crumple up your paper or shut your Mirror Pad and call it a day? "No way," the students of Ever After High say. Instead play hexciting story games or do brain-busting hexercises until the ideas flow like gooseberry tea at the Mad Hatter's Haberdashery and Tea Shoppe.

Ideas don't always come easy.

And just like the students at Ever After High all have their fave stories, they also have fave games. Curiouser and Curiouser what those games are? Turn another page and read on.

STORY SLAM

"My dad the White Rabbit was always hare-raisingly late no matter how many alarm clocks he got for his un-birthdays. That's why I, Bunny Blanc, am always a hop, skip and a jump away from being on time. That's right. I'm a time geek -- and proud of it!"

Bunny Blanc

That's why it's no surprise Bunny's favorite game is 'Story Slam' where storytellers have a short amount of time to tell a story.

To play, the storytellers are given a one-word theme like Magic, Crowns, Science, Crush, Travel. Then they get up one by one before a group of BFFA's to tell their story, from beginning to end, before their time is up. So don't forget to have a stopwatch or timekeeper nearby.

A Story Slam is an awesome game to play with story-loving friends. For Bunny, it's also a great way to make friends. Are you listening, Alistair Wonderland?

JUST WRITE!

"What does this reporter do when the words flow as slowly as week-old porridge? I don't get my locks in a twist, that's for sure. Instead I grin and bear it, then sit down with my quill or Mirror Pad and write, write – and write!"

Blondie Lockes

Writing might sound weird when the words won't come. But as Blondie agrees, sometimes writing something – anything – is better than writing nothing at all!

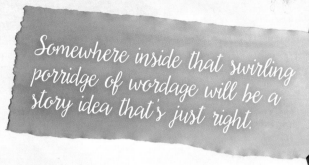

Somewhere inside that swirling porridge of wordage will be a story idea that's just right.

At first the words you come up with might be less than perfect. They may seem silly. Or boring. But somewhere inside that swirling porridge of wordage will be a story idea that's just right. And Blondie just happens to know a thing or two about just right!

So the next time when writing a story becomes a royal grind, do what Blondie Lockes does. Unlock the door to your spellbinding imagination and ...

JUST WRITE!

CHAIN STORY

"When the Charming family gets together we can hexpect a good time thanks to Grandpa and his crown-spinning games of chance and skill. As for me, my fave game isn't to build strength but to sharpen my storytelling chops. And with so many Charming cousins to go around, a 'Chain Story' is the way to go!"

Dexter Charming

The rules are fairy-easy: Get a group of friends or family members to sit in a line or circle. The first storyteller to go comes up with a Once Upon a Time, or the

ALWAYS BRAVE

beginning of the story. After only a few sentences, the next storyteller adds to the tale, then the next storyteller and the next and next until the last storyteller wraps it up with his own ending – or Happily Ever After.

Try Dexter's favorite storytelling game at your next party, sleepover or cousin convention. It's not just fun – it's totally off the book!

To get the juices flowing, a good chain story is the way to go!

33

REBEL REWRITE

"Okay, I admit I have serious destiny issues. Who wouldn't if their mom brought new meaning to the word wicked? I always wanted to rewrite my story, but until I decide what my new story will be – I practice by rewriting others!"

Raven Queen

Some of the most fableous stories to rewrite are the ones you know best. For Raven that would be fairytales. A rewritten fairytale is sometimes called a fractured fairytale. That's when you take a tale you know and change as much as you can about it: the characters, setting, plots, tone, even the time in which it takes place.

To write a fractured fairytale start by asking yourself 'what if?' What if Little Red Riding Hood and the Wolf teamed up to open a café called "Grandma's?" What if Prince Charming had a not-so-charming identical twin? What if all the girls in the kingdom wanted fashion-forward glass slippers like Cinderella's? What if Raven Queen woke up one morning with a fableous new destiny?

Rewritten stories don't have to be fairytales or stories in books. Try rewriting an episode of your fave TV show, maybe starring you. Or Raven's favorite, write a new lyric to a fresh beat.

To Raven Queen a whole new story is music to her ears. Which makes this hexercise wickedly charming!

HOW I ROLL

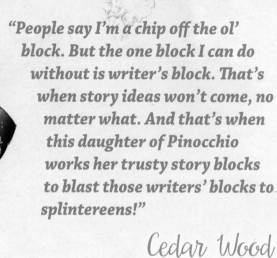

"People say I'm a chip off the ol' block. But the one block I can do without is writer's block. That's when story ideas won't come, no matter what. And that's when this daughter of Pinocchio works her trusty story blocks to blast those writers' blocks to splintereens!"

Cedar Wood

To make story blocks like Cedar's, grab a bunch of old toy blocks. Next paste or draw a different picture on all six sides. Make them totally random: a tumtum tree, crown, cup of cocoa, guitar, Tower Hair Salon, hedgehog – anything that pops into your head. When all sides are filled it's time to roll your blocks just like dice on a game board. The side that lands face-up will be the picture to build a story idea from.

The best part of this game is that you pull the strings. So if you don't like your idea keep rolling the blocks until you come up with one you do.

According to Cedar Wood, this game will set you on a roll with hexciting new story ideas in no time ... and that is no lie!

The best part of this game is that you get to pull the strings.

STORY IN THE SPOTLIGHT

"While dancing may be my destiny I also love a hint of ... drama! Drama is a fableous way to tell a story and brainstorm story ideas. And because I always love an audience, Story in the Spotlight is the perfect game for me."

Justine Dancer

To get started all you need is a friendly audience and two storytellers. The storytellers listen as friends toss out totally random words like spell, arrow, mirror or moat. After the storytellers agree on one word they have less than one minute to secretly figure out a scene to act out. Then it's show time as the storytellers perform an on-the-spot story without a single script.

In the world of drama that's called improvisation. To Justine it means, "Oh-my-Fairy-Godmother! I've got to think fast!"

STORY STARTER GRAB BAG

"*When it comes to traps, I've got an axe to grind. Trapped ideas can be worse than Pesky the squirrel throwing acorns at my head. Not cool! So when I need a quick story idea I reach into to my 'Story Starter Grab Bag'.*"

Hunter Huntsman

Hunter can build something out of anything. But a Story Starter Grab Bag can be built by anyone – and that includes you.

To begin all you need is a ready-made bag or pouch. Since bags were meant to be filled, hunt around your room or Enchanted Forest for random objects to use as story igniters.

Hunt around your room or Enchanted Forest for random story igniters.

When you have about a dozen objects, drop them into your bag. Then close it, shake it up good – and dig in. The object you pull out will be the one to brainstorm ideas from.

Got a key? Maybe it unlocks a mysterious trunk in the tower of your castle. A pair of crownglasses? What if those glasses saw into the future?

With a game like Story Starter Grab Bag you can forget about hunting high and low for an idea. It's in the bag!

THE BETTER TO HEAR YOU!

"Being the daughter of the Big Bad Wolf isn't always a picnic. You try hiding a pair of furry ears under a bright red hood every day. On the plus side it's my wolfy ears that give me special hearing powers. That's why, when it comes to storytelling games, my fave is 'The Better to Hear You!'

Cerise Hood

Here's how it works for Cerise: When she needs a story idea she secretly tunes in to a stranger's conversation at the Lifrairy, Muse-eum, sub-coach or anywhere in the hood. She then picks one overheard sentence and quickly builds a story around it.

For hexample, the other day when shopping at Spell Foods, Cerise heard a guy say, "I hate pickled pie." Right away she let her imagination fly to figure out why. Maybe in a previous life-story he fell into a giant pickled pie and had to eat his way out. Would that make a riddle-iculously good story? Write it and see. After all, big ears can lead to big ideas!

STORY SCAVENGER HUNT

"What's more awesome than writing a story straight from the heart? Sharing your story through a Story Scavenger Hunt. What makes it my fave storytelling game? One word: CARDS!"

Lizzie Hearts

Ready to get on deck and play too? Here's how:

If the storyteller is you, pick a story you wrote and want to share. Next, take about a dozen blank cards and line them up in a row. Starting with the first card, write a different part of your story on each from beginning to end. When all the cards are

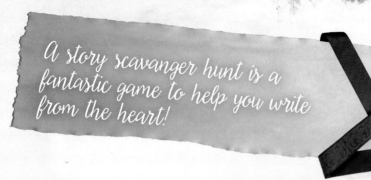

A story scavanger hunt is a fantastic game to help you write from the heart!

done, shuffle them well, then hide each one in different places around your room. Scatter around a few hints, too like riddles (Madeline Hatter's fave) or paper arrows (Hunter Huntsman's choice clue).

When all cards are out of sight, call in your BFFA's and let the Story Scavenger Hunt begin! Finding hidden cards is just the beginning. Once found it's up to your friends to line up the cards in order as they watch your tale unfold!

For Lizzie, this storytelling game is as cool as croquet. And if you don't agree, "Off with your head!"

BEST.WORST.DAY. EVER!

"So many parties, so little time – especially when your destiny means sleeping for a hundred years. To beat those ZZ's I throw the most spelltastic parties ever after. And since parties mean games – my favorite is a story game called, Best. Worst.Day.Ever."

Briar Beauty

The fun begins when one friend talks about an imaginary best day ever. Until another friend shouts, "Stop!" The storyteller must change the course of her story to make it the worst day ever – until someone yells, "Stop!" again. The storyteller keeps going, switching from best day ever to worst day ever each time a friend shouts, "Stop!"

As the "Stops" come faster and faster the switcheroo's become harder and harder. Until the storyteller herself yells, "Stop!" and the round is over.

Briar Beauty loves this game because she's always up for a good challenge – like staying awake all night at sleepovers. She also loves stories ... as long as they're not the bedtime kind!

EVER-AFTER-AWESOME STORY PROMPTS

Ready to practice your storytelling chops? Keep the following tales alive by deciding their destinies and writing what happens next ...

STORY PROMPT 1: *Rosabella Beauty is hexstatic to be holding Ever After High's first annual "Spelltacular Pet Contest." But hexcitement turns to chaos when Humphrey Dumpty's chicken King Benedict goes missing. Did Humphrey's feathery friend fly the coop? Was he a victim of fowl play? Think like a de-hex-tive and write this mystery!*

_____

_____

_____

_____

_____

_____

_____

_____

_____

_____

STORY PROMPT 2: *It's a bad hair day for Holly O'Hair, when sister Poppy gives her a hextreme makeover – and a shorter new 'do. What a day for Holly to also get locked up in a tower! Without her lengthy locks, how will this damsel in distress ever escape? Or will a hero save the day? You decide the 'write' ending!*

_____

_____

_____

_____

_____

_____

_____

_____

_____

_____

_____

_____

STORY PROMPT 3: *Dexter Charming is up for Grandpa Aloysius's new challenge: to capture a dragon and bring it back to the castle. He remembers to wear his armor -- but not his glasses. Is Dexter surprised when the dragon he snares is Raven Queen's pet dragon Nevermore! Dexter knows he's in royal trouble. But only you know what happens next!*

STORY PROMPT 4: *Ashlynn Ella is crown-over-heels. Her mom Cinderella is lending Ashlynn her famous glass slippers to wear to the Wonderland High Dance. But with the fableous shoes come Cinderella's Fairy Godmother – and that means a new rule. What is this new rule? And what happens at the dance when Ashlynn arrives?*

STORY PROMPT 5: *Blondie Lockes has one key that will open three doors: The first is painted strawfairy-red. The second is Baby-Bear-brown. The third door is covered with a sparkling crystal mirror. Which door does Blondie open first and what hexciting surprise lies behind it? Only you hold the key to her adventure!*

_____

_____

_____

_____

_____

_____

_____

_____

_____

_____

_____

STORY PROMPT 6: *Hats are flying inside the Mad Hatter's shop as Madeline preps for the most hextreme tea party. Thank madness for Kitty Cheshire dropping by to help brew the tea. But, instead of tea, Kitty brews her own prankish cups of spells – starting with a bubbly brew that shrinks Madeline to the size of a teabag! Is Madeline's party a cat-astrophe? Or just madder than ever? Put on your thinking-hat and write what happens next!*

_____

_____

_____

_____

_____

_____

_____

_____

_____

_____

_____

STORY PROMPT 7: *On their way to Lizzie Heart's croquet tournament, Alistair Wonderland and Bunny Blanc take an unexpected spill down a long, winding rabbit hole. What mad adventure is there to greet Alistair and Bunny down below? Is it Ever After Awesome?... Or Ever After Awful?*

STORY PROMPT 8: *When Briar Beauty is late for Storytelling 101 she misses her final hexam. Embarrassed to tell Mr. Nimble she overslept again, Briar concocts the most spelltastic story to hexplain why she's late – starting with a lovesick frog landing with a splash in her cereal bowl. Mr. Nimble loves a wild story – so grab a pen and finish Briar's!*

THE END

Congrats! Now you've got some tools and tips to write spelltastic stories of your own. But don't forget one of the most important ways to bubble up those creative juices – reading. Read all kinds of stories – mysteries and histories, tragedies and charmedies. Read the kind of stories you dream of writing yourself. And when that story 'Aha' moment hits and you're ready to write yourself, pick the ideal place to hocus-focus. Kitty Cheshire writes stories up in a tree. Madeline Hatter writes in a tea shoppe with a hat on her head and Earl Grey curled at her feet.

◇

What about you? Maybe a comfy corner of your room will do. Or at the library, surrounded by books for inspiration. Wherever or however you write your story it's what appears on the page that really, truly counts.

◇

So as this book ends may your Once Upon a Time begin.

Happy Writing!